D0899025

DISCARD

Westminster Public Library
3705 W 112th Ave
Westminster, CO 80031
www.westminsterlibrary.org

EDGE BOOKS

RECYCLED SCIENCE

AMAZING CARDBOARD TUBE SCIENCE

BY JODI WHEELER-TOPPEN

Consultant:
Marcelle A. Siegel
Associate Professor of Science Education
University of Missouri

CAPSTONE PRESS
a capstone imprint

Edge Books are published by Capstone Press,
1710 Roe Crest Drive, North Mankato, Minnesota 56003
www.mycapstone.com

Copyright © 2017 by Capstone Press, a Capstone imprint. All rights reserved. No part of this
publication may be reproduced in whole or in part, or stored in a retrieval system, or transmitted
in any form or by any means, electronic, mechanical, photocopying, recording, or otherwise,
without written permission of the publisher.

Library of Congress Cataloging-in-Publication Data
Names: Wheeler-Toppen, Jodi, author.
Title: Amazing cardboard tube science / By Jodi Wheeler-Toppen.
Description: North Mankato, Minnesota : Capstone Press, [2017] | Series: Edge
books. Recycled science | Audience: Ages 9–15.? | Audience: Grades 4 to 6.? | Includes
bibliographical references and index.
Identifiers: LCCN 2015045734|
ISBN 9781515708605 (library binding) |
ISBN 9781515708643 (eBook PDF)
Subjects: LCSH: Cardboard tube craft—Juvenile literature. |
Handicraft—Juvenile literature. | Recycling (Waste, etc.)—Juvenile literature. | Science—Study
and teaching—Juvenile literature.
Classification: LCC TT870 .W525 2017 | DDC 745.5—dc23
LC record available at http://lccn.loc.gov/2015045734

Editorial Credits
Brenda Haugen, editor; Russell Griesmer, designer; Tracey Cummins, media specialist;
Kathy McColley, production specialist

Photo Credits
Capstone Studio: Karon Dubke (All images except the following); Shutterstock: Georgios Kollidas, 23

Design elements provided by Shutterstock: bimka, FINDEEP, fourb, Golbay, jannoon028, mexrix,
Picsfive, Sarunyu_foto, STILLFX, Your Design

Printed and bound in the USA.
122016   10200R

TABLE OF CONTENTS

AMAZING CARDBOARD
TUBE SCIENCE

GET ROLLING!

Don't throw away that empty toilet paper roll! You have valuable scientific equipment in your hand! Why not try your hand at being a paper-tube engineer?

Like any engineer, you'll need to keep a few things in mind as you work. Sometimes, the first time you try a project, it doesn't work. Don't give up! Check over each part of your work to see if you can fix it. If you don't have all of the materials that a project requires, don't let that stop you either. See if you can redesign the project with materials you do have. And of course, follow all safety guidelines, and grab a grownup when you need one.

What are you waiting for? It's time to get rolling!

ABOUT CARDBOARD TUBES

This chapter divides cardboard tubes into long tubes and short tubes. Long tubes can come from a paper towel roll, a plastic wrap or aluminum foil container, or a wrapping paper tube that you have cut into pieces. Short tubes come from toilet paper rolls or long tubes that you have cut to about that size.

engineer—a person who designs, builds, and improves things

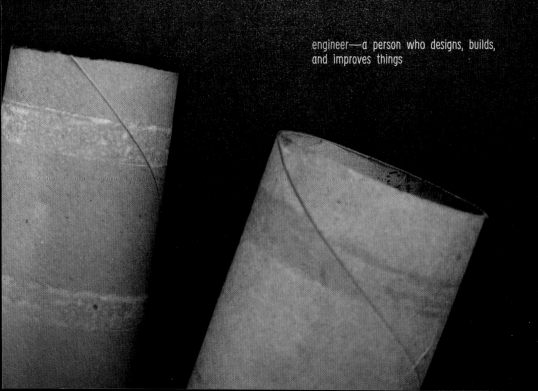

KAZOO

Place your hand on your throat and hum. Do you feel vibrations? Vibrations are the basis of sound. With this kazoo, you can enhance your humming vibrations and create a musical buzz.

SCIENCE BRANCH: PHYSICS
CONCEPT: ACOUSTICS

YOU'LL NEED:

- Long tube
- Ruler
- Rubber band
- Wax paper or plastic grocery bag
- Scissors
- Sharp pencil

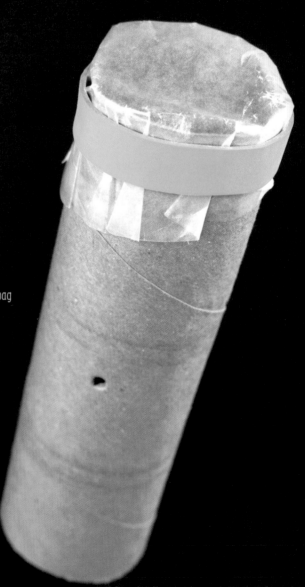

PUT IT TOGETHER:

STEP 1: Cut a 6-inch (15-centimeter) piece from a long tube.

STEP 2: Cut a circle about the size of a dessert plate from the wax paper or plastic bag.

STEP 3: Cover one end of your tube with the wax paper or plastic bag. Use the rubber band to hold it in place.

STEP 4: Use the sharp pencil to punch a hole in the middle of the top side of your tube.

STEP 5: Place the open end of the tube to your mouth.
Hum or sing using the sound "ta ta ta."
Experiment with high and low pitches.

REUSABLE KNOWLEDGE:

When you talk or sing, vibrations start in your larynx, which houses your vocal cords. The vibrations move into other parts of your throat and head. The vibrating body parts bump into air molecules. That starts the air molecules vibrating. When the vibrating air hits a person's eardrum, he or she hears your sound. Short, quick vibrations make a high pitch. Longer, slower vibrations make a low pitch.

With this kazoo, you send your vibrations through the air to the piece of wax paper or grocery bag. The air causes the paper or bag to vibrate. But it vibrates at a slightly different speed than your vocal cords. So the kazoo produces a sound that is similar, but not identical, to your hum.

vibration—rapid shaking back and forth

HOLE IN YOUR HAND

Your eyes and brain are usually pretty good partners. Your eyes collect light that reflects from the objects in front of you. They send the information to the brain for processing. The brain uses that information to recognize what you are seeing. With just a tube and your hand, however, you can get your eyes to send a message that will really confuse your brain.

SCIENCE BRANCH: **ANATOMY AND PHYSIOLOGY**
CONCEPT: **OPTICAL ILLUSIONS**

YOU'LL NEED:

– Paper towel tube
– Your hand

PUT IT TOGETHER:

STEP 1: With one hand, hold the paper towel tube up to your eye. Look through the tube as if you were looking through a telescope.

STEP 2: Hold the other hand up next to the tube, resting the side of your hand against the tube.

STEP 3: Stare straight ahead, and notice what you see. Make sure both eyes are open.

REUSABLE KNOWLEDGE:

Since your eyes are located about 2 inches (5 cm) apart, each one captures a slightly different image. Your brain overlaps the information from each eye to figure out what you are seeing. Usually your eyes see the same scene from a slightly different angle. Overlapping the two images gives you depth perception, or the ability to figure out how far away something is. In this activity, your brain follows its usual system of overlapping the two images, but they are of two different things. So you end up seeing a hole in your hand!

depth perception—being able to figure out how far away something is

ARE YOU RIGHT-EYED OR LEFT-EYED?

It is not just right-handedness and left-handedness that makes us different. You can also be right-eyed or left-eyed. Use a long tube to figure out which eye is your dominant eye, and shed some light on a mystery that has baffled scientists.

SCIENCE BRANCH: ANATOMY AND PHYSIOLOGY
CONCEPT: VISION

YOU'LL NEED:

- Long tube
- Wall with a light switch

PUT IT TOGETHER:

STEP 1: Grab a paper towel tube with both hands. Hold it in front of you with your arms stretched out.

STEP 2: Point the tube at a light switch or other small object on the wall. Back up until you can see the entire switch through the tube.

STEP 3: With your arms still extended, focus on the light switch. Without moving your body, close your left eye. Can you see the light switch through the tube?

STEP 4: Close your right eye, and open the left. Can you see the light switch now?

REUSABLE KNOWLEDGE:

Most people will hold the tube so that they see the light switch with only one eye. By closing one eye at a time, you can see which eye is lined up to view the switch. That is your dominant eye. As you saw in Hole in Your Hand (p. 8), both eyes send an image to your brain. Your brain usually combines the images. Sometimes, however, our brains pick the image from one eye over the image from the other. Scientists aren't sure why.

dominant eye—the eye favored by the brain in a given situation

MARSHMALLOW SHOOTER

Squeeze your arm muscles tight. Your muscles are full of energy. With this shooter, you can transfer some of that energy to a marshmallow and send it flying across the room. Ready. Aim. Fire!

SCIENCE BRANCH: PHYSICS
CONCEPT: ENERGY TRANSFER AND STORAGE

YOU'LL NEED:

- 2 short tubes
- 2 rubber bands
- Pencil
- Ruler
- Masking tape
- Scissors
- Hole puncher
- Large marshmallows

PUT IT TOGETHER:

STEP 1: Use the pencil to draw a 3/4-inch (2-cm) line straight down from the opening of one of your tubes. Draw a second line about a finger's width away. Cut along the lines to make two slits.

STEP 2: Make a second, identical pair of slits directly across the opening from the first pair. This will be your outer tube. Set it aside.

STEP 3: Use the scissors to cut a straight line along the length of the other tube, leaving it shaped like a hot dog bun.

STEP 4: Roll this tube until it is about half its original width. Tape it firmly. This will be your inside tube.

STEP 5: Make a pair of holes in the inside tube to hold your pencil. Punch one hole about 1 inch (2.5 cm) from the top on one side. Punch another hole directly across from it on the other side of the tube. Slide the pencil through the hole to make a handle.

STEP 2

STEP 3

STEP 6: Slide the inside tube into the outer tube. Make sure that the slits on the outer tube point away from the pencil.

STEP 7: Slide a rubber band into the pair of slits on one side. Hook the rubber band around the pencil on the same side. Repeat with the second rubber band on the other side.

STEP 9: To fire your shooter, stick a large marshmallow into the firing end. Grab the outer tube with one hand. It's OK if your hands are on top of the rubber band. Pull the handle back, and fire away!

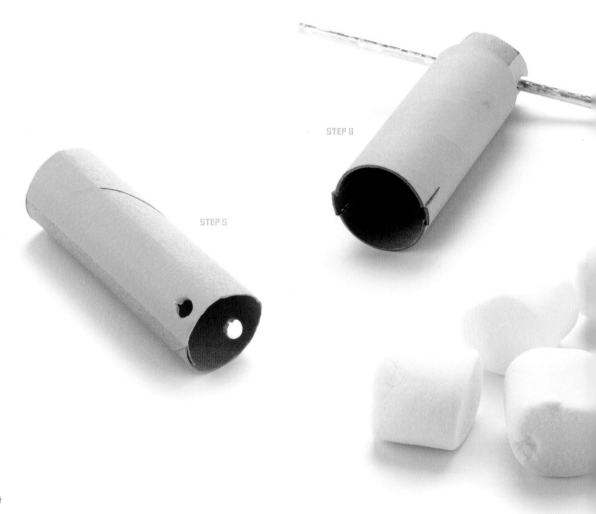

STEP 6

STEP 5

REUSABLE KNOWLEDGE:

When you use your shooter, you pass energy from your muscles to the rubber band to the marshmallow. You pull back the handle, and the rubber band stores some of the energy from your arm movement in its stretch. Scientists call this kind of stored energy potential energy because it has the potential to do work. Release the handle, and the rubber band springs into action. The stored energy becomes moving energy, called kinetic energy. The inside tube strikes the marshmallow, and it passes that kinetic energy on. Now the marshmallow has enough energy to fly across the room.

potential energy—energy stored in an object by stretching it, placing up high, or giving it electrical charge

kinetic energy—the energy possessed by an object due to its motion

MARBLE RUN

Hold a marble in your hand, and it doesn't seem like it has energy. But drop it in a marble run, and it speeds off. It even has enough energy to run uphill! Start by building the pieces described in the following experiment. Then design your own energy-releasing raceway.

SCIENCE BRANCH: PHYSICS
CONCEPT: GRAVITATIONAL POTENTIAL ENERGY

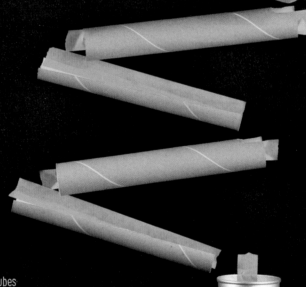

YOU'LL NEED:

- Long and short tubes
- Ruler
- Paper plate
- Soda can
- Masking tape
- Blue painter's tape
- Marbles

PUT IT TOGETHER:

STEP 1: First, create the pieces you will want to include in your design. To build a tunnel, cut a 1-inch (2.5-cm) U-shape out of the end of a tube so that a marble can drop in from above.

STEP 2: To create troughs, cut some of the tubes in half lengthwise. Each tube will give you two troughs.

STEP 3: To make an uphill bounce, take a trough made from a paper towel tube. Tape a piece of scrap paper to one end to form a wall. Arrange this piece so that the marble runs uphill, hits the wall, and heads back down.

STEP 4: To make a funnel, trace the bottom of a soda can in the center of a paper plate. Cut a straight line from the side of the plate to the circle you drew. Then cut out the circle. Hold the plate on either side of the straight cut. Overlap the sides to make a funnel. Tape the plate together in this position. Tape a tunnel to the bottom of the funnel to direct the marble into the next piece of your run.

TIP:

Painter's tape is designed to be removed from walls without tearing paint or wallpaper. Even with painter's tape, though, you should test it out before taping the whole run. Stick a piece of tape on an area that is not obvious. Then remove it to make sure that it will not mark up your wall.

STEP 1

STEP 2

STEP 5: Before you start to build your marble run, ask for permission to tape it to a wall or door using blue painter's tape.

STEP 6: Place the pieces you made in any order you like. As you add each piece, test your run. If the marble pops out of the track before it gets to the end, it is moving too fast. Slow it down by adding an uphill bounce or making the marble move in a straight line for a segment. You can also use tape to create walls or ceilings at places where the marble pops out.

STEP 7: Place the empty soda can upside down underneath the final part of your run to serve as an ending bell.

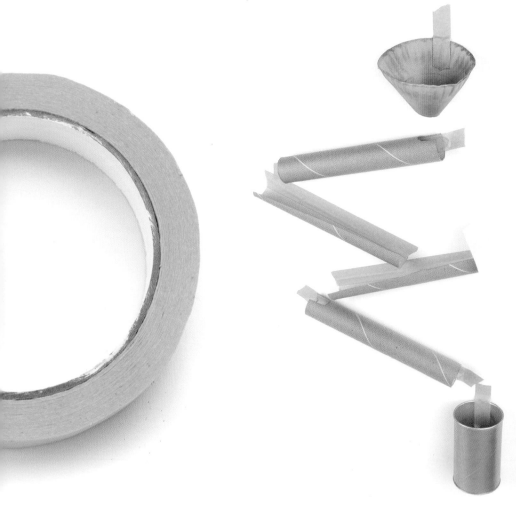

REUSABLE KNOWLEDGE:

A marble held up high has more energy than a marble sitting on the floor. How? You give it energy by lifting it up, against the force of gravity. Energy cannot be created or destroyed. It only moves from one object to another. The energy from your arm is transferred to the marble as potential energy. When you release the marble, gravity pulls it down. The potential energy turns into kinetic energy, just as it does with the marshmallow shooter. The higher you lift the marble, the more potential energy it has. As you can see with your uphill bounce piece, the marble even has enough energy to run uphill.

ON A ROLL

When you inflate a balloon, you use energy to stretch the rubber so it holds more air. The stretched rubber stores that energy, ready to force the air out as soon as it has a chance. Put your balloon's energy to work driving this recycled racecar.

SCIENCE BRANCH: PHYSICS
CONCEPT: NEWTON'S 2ND LAW OF MOTION

YOU'LL NEED:

- Ruler
- Short paper tube
- 2 pairs of matching bottle caps
- 2 straws
- Wooden skewer
- 2 large marshmallows
- Balloon
- Scissors
- Tape

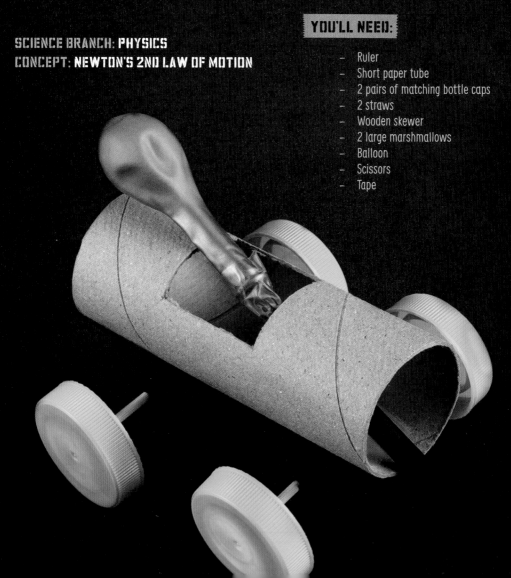

PUT IT TOGETHER:

STEP 1: Have an adult help you to cut two 4-inch (10-cm) lengths from the wooden skewer for axles.

STEP 2: Cut a large marshmallow in half. Press each half into one of your bottle caps, sticky side down. Repeat for the other two wheels.

STEP 3: Connect one set of wheels by sticking a skewer into the center of the marshmallows. Repeat for the other set.

STEP 4: Cut a square hole, about 1 1/2 inches (4 cm) wide, in the top of your paper tube.

STEP 5: Cut a straw into two 2-inch (5-cm) long pieces. These will hold the axles and wheels.

STEP 6: Flip the tube so that the square hole is facing down. Tape the pieces of straw across the bottom of the tube so that the wheels will stick off the side of the car. Make sure the straws are exactly parallel.

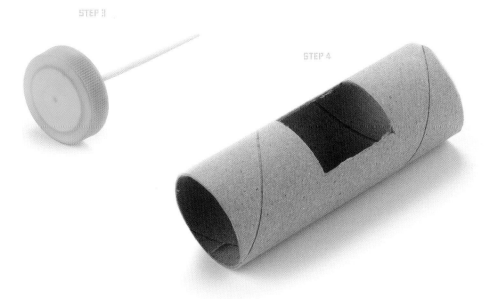

STEP 3

STEP 4

STEP 7: Attach the front wheels by removing one bottle cap from its skewer, sticking the skewer through the straw, and reattaching the wheel on the other side. Repeat for the back wheels.

STEP 8: Insert the second straw into the mouth of the balloon. Twist the balloon tightly, and tape it to the straw. Air should only be able to enter and leave the balloon through the straw.

STEP 9: Insert the straw into your square hole, and tape it so that end of the straw sticks straight out of the back of the car.

STEP 10: To make the car move, blow into the straw to inflate the balloon. Squeeze the end of the straw to hold the air in while you set the car on the ground and arrange the wheels.

STEP 11: Release your grip, and the car should roll across the ground.

STEP 8

STEP 7

STEP 10

REUSABLE KNOWLEDGE:

In the 1600s a scientist named Isaac Newton said that for every action, there is an equal and opposite reaction. When you release the balloon, the stretched rubber pushes the air out. At the same time, the air pushes back against the balloon with an equal force. Since the balloon is attached to your car, the air pushes the car forward. This is the same principle that allows rockets to take off. A rocket engine pushes hot gases down. At the same time, those gases push back against the rocket and lift it into space.

FLASHLIGHT

Like everything else in the universe, metal
wires are made up of atoms. Atoms are made
of particles called electrons, protons, and
neutrons. If you get the electrons in atoms
moving, you've got electricity. In this activity,
you will build a circuit to move electrons and
light up a flashlight.

SCIENCE BRANCH: **PHYSICS**
CONCEPT: **ELECTRICAL CIRCUITS**

YOU'LL NEED:

- Long tube
- Old string of holiday lights with
  the plug removed
- Ruler
- 2 C batteries
- Masking tape or electrical tape
- Paper clip
- 2 brads
- Wire cutter and stripper
- Hole punch
- An adult to help you

PUT IT TOGETHER:

STEP 1: Have an adult use the wire cutters to cut one bulb from the string of holiday lights. Leave as much wire as possible on either side of the bulb.

STEP 2: Have an adult strip about 1 inch (2.5 cm) of plastic coating from the wire on one end of the bulb. Repeat for the other side of the wire.

STEP 3: There will be at least one long wire in the light set that does not connect to the bulbs. Have an adult use wire cutters to cut three lengths from this wire, each about 8 inches (20 cm) long. Have the adult strip 1 inch (2.5 cm) of coating from both ends of each wire. These will be your long wires.

STEP 4: Test your light bulb. Touch the two wires attached to the bulb to either side of one of your batteries. If you are using LED bulbs, electricity can only flow one way through them, so you may have to try reversing which side of the battery meets which wire. The bulb should light up. If you cannot get it to light up, repeat Step 1 to find a working bulb.

STEP 2

STEP 4

STEP 5

TIP:

Most holiday lights will fit into the wire stripper slots for 20 or 22 AWG.

atom—the basic building block of all matter

electron—negatively charged particle in the nucleus of an atom

proton—positively charged particle in the nucleus of an atom

neutron—particle in the nucleus of an atom that has no electric charge

circuit—the path that electricity follows

STEP 5: Lay out your batteries so that the positive terminal (the bump) on one end meets the negative terminal (the flat end) of the other. Tape the batteries firmly, making sure the ends stay pressed together. This is your battery pack. Test your bulb against the two exposed sides. If it does not light, tape the batteries more tightly.

STEP 6: Take one of your long wires and attach it to one end of your bulb by twisting the exposed metal ends together. Secure the connection by taping it with masking tape or electrical tape. Repeat, adding another long wire to the other side of your light bulb. Once again, touch the wires to the battery pack to make sure your connections are good.

STEP 7: Punch a hole about 1/2 inch (1.3 cm) from the end of your tube. Punch another hold opposite the first. Thread the wires on either side of the light bulb through the holes so that the bulb is centered at the end of your tube.

STEP 8: On the opposite end of the flashlight, punch one hole about 1 inch (2.5 cm) from the end. Measure 1 inch (2.5 cm) from the first hole, and punch a second hole. To make this punch, you will need to squeeze the side of the tube to make a fold, and then punch half a circle into the fold.

TIP:

The sturdier the tube, the better. Cardboard tubes from inside aluminum foil and wax paper are often stronger than those from paper towels.

terminal—the positive or negative connection point on a battery

STEP 9

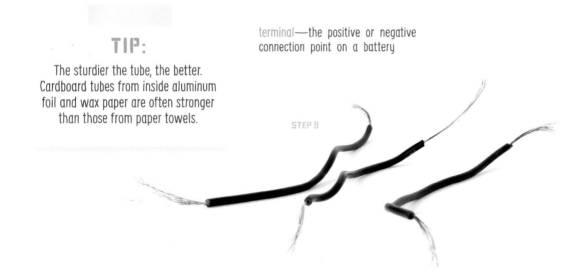

STEP 9: Wrap the exposed wire from one side of your bulb around the top of a brad. Insert the brad into one of holes. Reach inside the tube, and open the legs of the brad so it stays in place.

STEP 10: Take the long wire that you have not yet used. Wrap one end of around the second brad. Slip the paper clip onto the brad, and insert the brad into the second hole. Open the legs of the brad to hold it in place.

STEP 11: Tape the wire coming from the brad to the center of one terminal on your battery pack. Tape the remaining wire from the light bulb to the center of the other terminal of your battery pack.

STEP 12: To turn the flashlight on, twist the paperclip so it touches both brads. To turn the flashlight off, twist the paperclip so that it does not touch the second brad.

STEP 11

REUSABLE KNOWLEDGE:

Electrons move from areas with a negative charge to areas with a positive charge. Each battery has a negative end and a positive end. When you connect batteries with wires, electrons move from one side to the other. Stick a light bulb along that path, and the electrons will light it up as they move. This is called an electric circuit.

It's no accident that the word circuit sounds like circle. To keep the electrons moving, you need a complete circle from one battery terminal to the other. If you twist the paperclip so that the wires are no longer connected, you create an opening in the path. Electricity cannot flow. This is called an open circuit. To get electricity moving again, you must connect the paperclip and close the circuit. Then the bulb lights up.

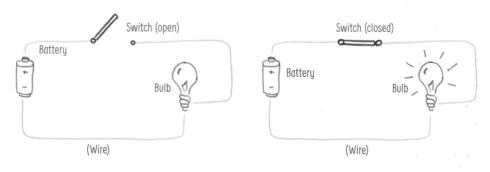

Switch (open)   Switch (closed)

Battery   Battery

Bulb   Bulb

(Wire)   (Wire)

PLANTABLE PLANTER

Inside a tiny grass seed is a plant embryo and a store of food to help it grow. When the seed is soaked in water, that's the new plant's cue to press its way out and sprout. Use a short tube to create a cute container for your sprouting seeds, and then plant them—box and all—in your yard.

SCIENCE BRANCH: BIOLOGY
CONCEPT: SEEDS AND SPROUTS

YOU'LL NEED:

- Ruler
- Short tube
- 1 teaspoon of grass seed
- 3/4 cup (177 grams) of potting soil
- Magic markers
- Scissors

PUT IT TOGETHER:

STEP 1: Draw four 1-inch (2.5-cm) lines at equal distances around one end of your tube. Cut along each line to make four small flaps.

STEP 2: Fold the flaps so that each flap overlaps the one before it. Tuck one side of the last flap under the first flap. Press the flaps tightly to make a flat bottom for your planter.

STEP 3: Using the magic markers, draw a face on each planter.

STEP 4: Fill the planter 3/4 full of potting soil. Spread the seeds on top of the soil. Add a thin layer of soil to cover the seeds.

STEP 5: Water the seeds, but be careful not to add so much water that the roll is drenched.

STEP 6: Place your planter in a warm place. Keep the soil moist but not soaked. Your seeds should sprout hair in 5 to 14 days.

STEP 7: Plant your sprouts, tube and all, in a bald spot in your lawn.

STEP 4

STEP 2

TIP:

Set your planter on a plate to catch any dirty water that might leak from the bottom.

REUSABLE KNOWLEDGE:

Even inside a seed, the embryo has a top and a bottom. One end is set to become roots. The other will become a stem. But you don't have to worry about planting your seeds upside down. Plants sense gravity. Roots and stems will turn to grow in the right direction. A bonus to starting seed in this planter is that it will break down in the ground and become soil. You won't even have to disturb your sprouts to move them to your lawn.

embryo—the portion of a seed that will grow into a plant

atom—the basic building block of all matter

circuit—the path that electricity follows

depth perception—being able to figure out how far away something is

dominant eye—the eye favored by the brain in a given situation

electron—negatively charged particle in the nucleus of an atom

embryo—the portion of a seed that will grow into a plant

engineer—a person who designs, builds, and improves things

kinetic energy—the energy possessed by an object due to its motion

neutron—particle in the nucleus of an atom that has no electric charge

potential energy—energy stored in an object by stretching it, placing up high, or giving it electrical charge

proton—positively charged particle in the nucleus of an atom

terminal—the positive or negative connection point on a battery

vibration—rapid shaking back and forth

READ MORE

Enz, Tammy. *Repurpose It: Invent New Uses for Old Stuff.* Invent It. North Mankato, Minn.: Capstone Press, 2012.

Slade, Suzanne. *Cool Physics Activities for Girls.* Girls Science Club. North Mankato, Minn.: Capstone Press, 2012.

Walker, Sally M., and Roseann Feldmann. *Put to the Test: Wheels and Axles.* Experiments with Simple Machines. Minneapolis: Lerner Publications Co., 2012.

INTERNET SITES

FactHound offers a safe, fun way to find Internet sites related to this book. All of the sites on FactHound have been researched by our staff.

Here's all you do:
Visit *www.facthound.com*
Type in this code: 9781515708605

Check out projects, games and lots more at
www.capstonekids.com

Super-cool stuff!

CRITICAL THINKING USING THE COMMON CORE

1. The introduction to the activity on page 10 suggests that there is a mystery related to this activity that scientists haven't figured out. Why do you suppose the author waited until the end of the activity to tell what the mystery was? (Integration of Knowledge and Ideas)

2. This book uses both pictures and words to give directions. Pick one of the activities to consider. What information can you get from the pictures that you don't get from the words? What is told in words that is not shown in pictures? (Craft and Structure)

3. When you flip a light switch and turn the light on, are you opening or closing the circuit? Use specific information from Flashlight, beginning on page 24, to support your answer. (Integration of Knowledge and Ideas)

INDEX